For Chris and Kim
Louise Colln

TIME REMOVED

By Louise Colln

Ideas into Books: Westview®
Kingston Springs, Tennessee

Ideas into Books®
W E S T V I E W
P.O. Box 605
Kingston Springs, TN 37082
www.publishedbywestview.com

ISBN 978-1-62880-161-3

First edition, October 2018.

Cover photo by Claire Henry.

The author gratefully acknowledges permission from George Spain to quote from his book *Dreaming the Fire Away*.

Printed in the United States of America on acid free paper.

Other books by Louise Colln

Mountain House
A Place For Love
Falling Water Valley
Birdsong Road
Cassie's River Walk
Woman Of The Land: Mary, Mother of The Christ
The Women of Rogers Street
War Trees

Acknowledgements

Thank you to the following publishers

One: Jacar Press – "Evening At Fox Hollow Inn"
POEM – "Michael Searching" –"Promises"
Muscadine Lines - A Southern Anthology – "Upcountry South
    Carolina Homecoming"
Our Voices Williamson County Literary Review 1978 – "Laura,
    After Dying" -
Voices Poems From The Missouri Heartland – "Silence" –
    "Perspective"

I would send a new poem to Nancy Fletcher-Blume and she would
say "I like it but this stopped me" and we would work on a word
or a line. Thank you, Nancy.

Heartfelt thanks to Victoria Clausi, Catherine Moore, Sally Lee,
and Claire Henry for the time and care they have given me.
Thanks to George Spain for his support and help, especially with
"The Death Of Eve". Thank you, Jerry Henderson, for the title
and your support. Thanks to the Wednesday Morning Writer's
Group, The Women Writers, the Saturday Morning Poetry
Critique, the Seventh Street Poetry Group, the Saturday Morning
Critique Group and especially to Susie Margaret Ross for your
written notes.

Contents

To Every One I Ever Loved

Time

Time tumbles about in a mortal mind
Like an unrolling ball of yarn.
Picked up and rewound
Yesterday becomes today,
Tomorrow rules the troubled night.

Time reincarnates the wind whistling
Across the mouth of a cave
Where the Old Ones sleep in furs
Or on naked stone,
The congregated mobile tents
Of camel riders, reindeer herders,
The cold camp space
Of Genghis Khan or Jesus,
And around the cabins
Of lonely pioneers.

Time locks us in
Slammed shut against the knocks of friends,
Or shoves us out
To dance a reel with strangers.

Time is filled with streaks of kindness. It promises
We will love the world together
And the world will love us back
In time.
Old wounds will heal.
In time
We will learn of war no more.
We'll sing with the bluebird.

I may have written a poem

I may have dug into my soul
And found chunks of wisdom to fling at you
I may have hung white linens on a line
To guide you home
or
I may have
Made a pasted ball of words
To throw
     for the dog
         to retrieve.

Dandelion Wine

And love your neighbor as yourself

I brought my neighbor to my house. I led her to my chair. I prepared for her a bowl of soup for comfort in her sorrow. We shared our language voices.

I filled her glass with dandelion wine and spoke to her of strength to come from it, for dandelions are the strongest of flowers. Ignoring their unpopularity they simply grow, their thick tough stems and very yellow crowns stand tall above grass lawns and concrete cracks. And when they are old only children will swirl their white heads.

I loved myself for loving her until doubt drifted in. How many dandelions need I pick to distill one more glass of wine for my sorrowing neighbor? How many hours must I spend on my knees?

After Reading My Grandmother's Old Letters

When they found each other
they had already created
lives that kept their lives apart.
Only once they let a strange river
float them round its sweet curves,
while God or the Devil gently drew them on,
till they felt fishes nibbling their bodies
and returned to their safe banks.
Through summer's green heat or winter's white cold
she barely touched the memory in her letters;
a word, a phrase here and there
she thought only he would recognize.
How could she know
her granddaughter would float that same sweet river?

Queen Substance

As the worker bees gather about the queen
stroking themselves against her body,
bonding her chemical element;
creating their hive;
I gather myself about you,
stroking my body to yours,
accepting your sweat
into my pores,
sharing your breath.
Your fingers touch
like teasing wings;
your tongue, your lips,
your gentle teeth
surrender me joyously
to your queen substance;
pouring your life
into mine,
creating our one.

Last Year At Roaring River

These two,
One slowed by bitter nature, one who chose to wait,
Acknowledge mountain tops beyond their reach
So walk the valley.
Rest often.
Watch riffles in the stream,
Till eyes track shadows in the depth
Reflecting darkness on the mountain rim.
In walnut shade see lace against the sky.
Lay bets on which fall first, a leaf or nut,
Do not say
This last time.
Both know.

After Reading His Writing

Reading his writing
now
tears out her heart
with longing
for something with no
name.
It lingers in the loving
part of her mind.

That year
new green leaves fell
like autumn's litter.
Wind turned summer trees back
To naked winter limbs.
The sun
was covered,
making twilight
for owls to fly in.
Morning.
Noon.
Night.
Hooting.
Hooting.
Hooting.
Flowers forgot to bloom
for bees to work the world
back to life.

Frightened
of the silent future
She turned away.
Love left.
No dreams bring it back.

Time Removed

I did not choose to be
moved about your world;
a pawn in your evening game
of chess with your adversary
which you almost always win,
until I arrived at the place
you wanted me, where the one I
was meant to love lived. Later
I walked alone even with others near
and sighed. But now in time removed
I'm glad to have been that pawn
in your evening game of chess,
which you almost always win.
Tonight, name the game for me.

Bond

You are my love and I will
not leave You. I will cling to
Your hand. If a wind sucks me away
I will fly to You above the deep water
which pulls me to its peace and blanket of coolness.
Your soft arms turn me around to face where my soul lies
meaning my soul lies with no truth except I will not leave You.
I will not leave You though You send me away.
Remember me.

I Am the Prostitute

I am the prostitute who knelt before his feet.
Poor tired feet,
nails too long or broken;
I trimmed them with my stone
and buffed away a callus
on his toe.
I stroked each toe, massaged
the red, raw places.
I know massage that's how I make my money
caressing drunken soldiers.
My tears poured down to wash away the sand
embedded in the creases of his skin,
my hair grew long to be his drying towel.
I washed his feet.

The Christ of the Bloody Fields

He walks
Across the battle detritus,
Picks up a child's doll
And puts it in his pocket.
It will surprise her in heaven.
And a child's foot,
Softly cuddled in a mother's hand
Just an hour ago,
He carries to the body,
Still nestled closely in her dead arms.
He lets his bare feet feel sharp edges
And bleeds again.

Time Removed

somewhere beyond

in a timeless twilit nowhere
we lie breast to breast

through the universes
we were children
before the clash of planets
of earth and ashes
Unknowing

where the path of time shifts
downward
we spend time together
whispering words kept secret
for each other
of mist and light
together in the darkness
in flaming fiery joining
creating a world
Unfinished

Until then

Reawakening One

You ask me what I want from you
I say, *Just be my friend,*
And know I lie;
That in some ancient universe
We were more than friends,
More than lovers.
Perhaps we were gods.
Perhaps we killed each other,
Leapt down together to the deep,
Rolled in twisting, biting love,
Then kissed good-bye
Until the next life.

The Death of Eve

God, Lord, Father,
I stand in the doorway of leaving.
Breath is leaving my body.
Wisdom and her wise women gather round me.

I have lived eons since we stumbled from the garden
barefoot,
wearing only animal furs,
with the fire at our backs,
into the vine covered wilderness;
wild and beautiful in its wildness.
We have learned to weave grasses into cloth to cover us;
so we and animals can live in peace together.
Someday, perhaps, we will.

I have been chained to my choice
these yearning years.
My guilt follows me—the story of Your curse
which has become a blessing;
tears, wife, mother, worker, happy, crying,
cared for, caring, loved, lover, woman.
Father, Lord, God, did You know
Your curse would make me whole?
That it would let me grow from the girl
who could only dance and frolic
among the flowers?

I have suffered, I have fallen,
but I have not failed.
I am mother.

I did not know death
until I discovered birth,
and the feelings of a mother;
feelings that blur my brain and fill my heart with softness
for each tiny person who will become a woman or a man;
the cherished child who grows in me,
feeding from my body.
My Lord, the miracle.
You gave me daughters and sons
who married each other,
and taught me love for children many times removed.
We have replenished the earth
with fighting, drinking, loving, righteous, men and women
who choose to love You and each other.
An observation, my Lord;
You created us male and female,
made to fit our differences together
one's strength into the weakness of the other,
filling our spaces
to make us one.
We do in our way
but, oh,
we tear against each other
at the edges.
Only love stitches us together,
walking between happiness and sorrow.

We wonder. Why? Why?
Why were we created?
Are we made to adore You,
and fight Lucifer, that bright morning angel?
Are we Your blunted swords in that fight,
as we were in the garden?
Who knows Your plans?

I linger, in my last minutes.
My Lord, forgive me, though I question.
I feel that last deep breath,
in my heavy body.
It is enough, I step through the doorway.
But…..what? I float…. I fly…
I see a light!
What makes this lovely light
which woke the dawn of life so long ago?
The colors, and the soothing softness
of grass and air…

It is the garden!
It is the garden!
My Lord, my God!
It is the garden!

You lead me to the trees.
The trees of wisdom and life
intertwine their branches.

I stand
in their shade.

Shadows

The shadow on the sundial
May tell the span of love.

Black pencil paints of spider limbs
on snow are nature's winter gifts
filling the soul to serenity.

Living inside a chosen cavern
makes shadows cast outside
that spiritual pothole
become the real world.

I knew a child,
of ancient years though young
who created shadows to carry
heavy on fragile shoulders
until they crumbled.

Shadows move without reason
To trip frail feet on a trusted path.
They lean to the ground
from trees which never grew.
Unreal they stretch
from memories of one soul
to the heart of another.

The shadow of a falling leaf
speaks of reawakening.
Circling.

After Reading A Book of Poetry

He speaks of love…
nature…
animals…
one woman…two…
filling his life;
yet there are words…
phrases…showing…
a deep heart lonely
that no love can reach,
no presence comfort,
no touch massage,
though pleasure may mask pain
and love make heaven
for a while.
I read his words
and wander with him
in the sun-dry desert,
chewing dried goat flesh,
searching for a burning bush
or a flaming throne.

Beyond The Hills

The owl rules the night.
Its hoots send me
riding my black mare across
the dream hills,
in thin strips of rags
that barely cover my body;
my bare legs whipping
the mare's sides as I urge it on.

Beyond the hills
there is a man of darkness
who tells me a story
never told before.
He says to bury it
deep in my soul
and keep it there
unshared.
It rests there
its presence known
its reality
not remembered.

Reawakening Two

Let us find our bones in the mountain,
Where we lie each with the sword of the other,
Plunged in some Celtic battle
In the void where our hearts used to be.

Let us see me on the Devil's black altar,
Where you in your robes held the knife,
Then understanding my spirit
Carried me home to your cell.

Let us lie where the shore loves the ocean,
Feel the wandering waves of the water,
When wantonly we danced together
Naked across the sand.

Let us live here between the rivers
In the land that once was Eden,
Sweat over our corn and barley,
Go tired to our loving bed.

A Love Letter From Here

There was a time when love filled my days,
my noons, my nights, my air,
my spirit, my soul, the beats
of my heart. I would never go from You;
but Your love frightened me.
Perhaps mine wearied You.
I have tried past time, to hold love,
not knowing. Are You there
to be loved from here?
It is 167 steps to the altar to take
Communion. To accept the
blood of Christ shed for me.
Is it the same as the altar
where I laid the life I lived?
The nights move on dark dreams.

They tell of time spinning itself out

without recompense, only loss

of a voice that held comfort or pain

both saved

in a secret drawer now lost.

The dark shadow of wide wings

moves across the earth.

Will the wings deliver—will You accept—

my love letter to You

from here?

When The God Plays

Venus and Aphrodite
Battled through my night.
As I slept and dreamed
They touched my thigh with lucent hands,
And broke my bones.

At dawn they know that they are one.
Snake-wound they returned
To their ancient sea.

And as they left;
With twining arms
They tore the pillars from my mind,
Wrapped me in the luring gaze
Of Bacchus's beautiful eyes.

I Did Not Fall In Love

I did not fall in love. No, I did not fall in love. I was surrounded by love. I sank inside love. I lived in love without knowing that I moved in love's aura. Love had no beginning. It was a mist around me, a mist through which I walked; that swirled around my legs, massaged my body, entranced my mind, infiltrated my spirit. It had no beginning. It was. No, I did not fall in love. Love fell into me.

You Came Back Today

You came back today.
No questions now
Of where or why
Or will you stay.
And I won't say
What trails I took,
Who eased my loss,
Nor name the waters
That slipped like silk,
Or bucked and banged,
Beneath the bridges
I walked across,
While you were away.

Love Doesn't Always Lift Us Up

I knew a woman
who loved
a man
not wisely,
for by chance,
or by choice,
he left.
Her face came apart
we called it wrinkles, but
I could see infinitesimal
space between the cells
and in her deepest core
something lay down
and never moved again.

When I Call Your Name

I need to call your name
sometimes
when I am alone,
to see again your face,
to know still your touch,
or thoughts tossed-mind-to-mind
in our talk times—searched in my memories.
There is the shadow of a sharp sword.
It shapes my life before and after
that misunderstood moment
in another sweet universe
made of grace and pain.
I drift there
when I call your name.

Last Evening, After Loving

Last evening, after loving, you touched my face and laid
your hand on mine, between us. You turned to look
into the tree that lets its leaves brush gently
across our window. I saw a touch, a flash,
of the young person you used to be
flow across your softened face.
It drifted off. I turned it loose.
Loving the youth of then,
loving the you of now,
I watched you sleep.

Clouds Spread Wide Like Wings

And when I entered heaven
my friend, Saint Peter, hugged me;
met in the jade years, the hasty years,
when children played and evening dark
was brighter than morning light.

He said, "And didst thou die in doubt?
Look back one time, before I close the gate
dear doubting soul, spirit torn when God,
or Satan, rode His red, red horse.

And didst thou die in sadness?
Look back one time, before I close the gate."
Your voice spread through the fields of heaven,
a thread through hope, turned grief,
turned anger, not yet forgotten, when God,
or Satan, rode His ashen horse,
spread earth across the sky
of heaven. That sky is
soft with angel clouds
swept wide like wings.

"And didst thou die in sorrow
beneath the moving shade of the bright bird,
singing too high of love above you?
Look back one time, before I close the gate."

I followed you. You looked beyond,
drinking the whiskey of hope
that your love would return,
yet I took your hand.
I walked alone beside you,
and my footsteps turned to music,
and the music understood.

"Look up dear friend,"
the good Saint said,
"before I close the gate
for thou didst die in love."

Two Came By

A sudden tissue cloud,
A marshmallow mist;
Unused to her new self
She came to a precipitous landing
Against my shoulders.
Oh, I said,

You startled me.
She didn't stay.

Like the earlier one,
Who died before his body died
So left without goodbye,
Came quietly one day
Into my space.
He didn't stay.

Perhaps I missed a message
But their presence sufficed.

Promises

If I can find my comfort place
Within your loving arms,
I'll wrap me up and rest.
We'll consider Granny's garden
How she hoed and raked the ground,
Planted straight by strings and stakes
In rows from North to South,
Peas, cabbages and cucumbers,
Potato eyes buried in the old of the moon,
Four corn kernels in each covered hill,
And, beside her country road,
Two rows of yellow daisies.
Then we'll plant our soft leaved milkweed
Criss-curved about our grotto,
And watch each pinstriped caterpillar
Wrap its secret inner core
Wait there in its cave of life —
Trembling,
Surprised,
Unfolding wings.

On A Slow Dripping Morning

On a slow dripping morning
I want to shout to the clouds
If you're going to rain get on with it
One drop per minute does nothing.
I move away from the window
Walk from room to room
Eat a handful of peanuts
Watch a handful of news.
I think of hoarders,
An article I read yesterday
About keeping boxes
Of old things; handkerchiefs, blouses.
Afraid that letting one thing go
Will let some loved thing/person/hope
Drift from the tubercles of the mind.
As if that being accepts lying in sealed boxes.
I say to myself that in my several moves
To several homes, items slide off me
Like leaves in autumn.
And then I remember
That in a bottom drawer in my kitchen
Is a tangle of keys
To every door I ever locked.
And in a cupboard is a statue,
With the bat broken off,
Awarded to my dead son as a teenager.

Poetry Doesn't Keep Secrets

After reading your poem
in a borrowed book, I know
the thing, the dismal something,
that walks through your room in the night,
throws you down and chokes you until it hears
the silent scream you throw against the sodden wall
between you and all the universe of heaven;
the truth you wouldn't tell me if I asked.
I know knowing will make me cry
for the love you can't offer
from your shattered heart
to the person you love.
Poetry will do that.
Poetry tells your mysteries,
Poetry is pitiless to your soul.
Poetry digs deep into your center
and pulls out words that tells your truth
to anyone who reads with simple understanding;
if you are in love and if you are loved back,
your yearnings, thoughts. No matter
how carefully you have sewn
words over words to cover
yourself in fine robes,
poetry will send you
naked in the street.

Michael, Searching

When they said six months to a year
He bought a red convertible
And drove too fast down dim country roads
With the top down,
Even in the rain.

He went to concerts
And lived the music all night long,
Letting it wrestle with him
And dislocate his thighbone.

When they said six months, perhaps,
He went to the mountains
With someone whose name he didn't speak,
Even when his muscles needed help,
And he was carried beyond the trail.

He found an old friend
Spent a night of love.
And didn't say good-bye.

When they said three months
He went to live in the woods
By a stream that braided over sharp, white, rocks.
He skipped smooth stones across the water
Even when it snowed.
He built a rounded icon
To watch it melt.

He didn't take his body in
For the last evaluation,
Ignoring their carefully worded requests.

All year he called God out.
God met him by the first windflower.

Remembering

I wish we had made a pact to meet somewhere...
after the marriages...children...careers...
heart wounds healed...
at six o'clock on a certain day... in a certain park...
you know the one.

I want to know you now;
sit silent holding caring hands...
as two who spent long years together...
then lay us down to sleep...home at last...

Upcountry Carolina Homecoming

Cousins, kissing,

talk and listen

on parallel tiers,

in acappella roundelay.

Matching syllable to syllable,

they sew words lightly,

soul warming pieces of patchwork quilts

stitched together with hugs.

They discuss ancestors as part of present lives; "Great-grand-
daddy met Great-grand-mama at Seneca in nineteen ought four."
They dissect dour sepia pictures for forehead and lips, lay fingers
across chins and noses; "See that mouth, that's James. There's
Great-grand-daddy, for sure, there in Tommy's eyes."

Conversation boils

like cresting cusps of mountain rivers;

tongues curl richly around native names,

Tugaloo…Toccoa…Wakulla…Walhalla…Nantahala…

Swannanoa…Tuckasegee…Keowee…

Crooning tones

blend with shade-tree music

of flat top guitar, banjo, fiddle,

clacking spoons, and clogging feet

on squares of wood. Sweet dulcimers sing

above the feathery squeals of playing children.

Mothers smile.

"Honey, just mash that light on for me, where's grand-mama, oh, she had to go make a branch, never mind, you might could put more Ritz crackers in that macaroni and cheese pie, m-m-m don't that smell good, though?"

Kitchen smells,

biscuits, chicken, ham,

barbecue,

swirl out to gladdened noses,

braiding and unbraiding with scents

of hibiscus, gardenias, purple thrift, roses,

creamy lilies.

Old horseshoe pitchers

under the chinaberry tree

pause and think eagerly

of the feast to come after the blessing.

They laugh about their long childhood wait

for the old-timey preacher

to bless the children

bless the green grass,

bless the blue sky,

bless the (cooling) food to our (hungry) bodies.

The old men bless the young minister

who sends God a short e-mail

instead of an epistle.

They speak briefly, with lowered lids, of emotional blessings, of children, of wives, "That grand-son of mine is a pistol, all right." Then they pick up horseshoes again, looking kindly at the one who stands in silence, remembering grief.

Half-focused on target stakes,

leaners, ringers,

they listen for the signal

to break bread together with kinfolk;

savor already

respect due and given to the elders of the clan,

there at the long table.

Upcountry Carolinians

are huggers, touchers, givers,

dancers, singers, fighters, drinkers,

hunters, tellers of stories, lovers

of God and guns,

children and country,

of women

and fierce freedom-fighting men

in time misted Scots tartans,

yesterday's gray homespun,

and today's camouflage.

Upcountry Carolinians

are people-minded,

mountain-minded.

Beloved…

Old House On A Deep Mountain Road

Friend to dogs,

                cows and mules,

it had fire places,

      sleep places,

               cook places,

                      enough for a good hard life.

A river

             runs

     beside

   the   road.

It's last name is Fork.

It's first name is Caney or Jakes or Clines.

       It   curls

  around the rocks   like a lover.

       Hear you!

Your ancestors lived here.

               Fought,

                  plowed.

                    planted;

loved after working.

  Put aside your DNA.

               There is a link

beyond flesh on bones.

Perspective

You say
grief eases when a year has passed. I'll stop
thinking, *This time last year…*
I find that true. But many years won't bring
another, who, when I say that I may choose
to disbelieve the new honed verity
that wolves won't harry humans,
rather than lose the awed-child thrilling, chill
of bridal parties pulled by wild-eyed, foaming,
horses across a frozen Russia, thrown one
by one to ground for evil beasts to eat;
and patient, red-rimmed, lustful eyes
circling wood starved fires;
will only nod and smile,
not needing to ask *Why*
nor offer me a grim-eyed chase
in crashing cars through city streets
instead.

Birth Of a Poem

Perhaps there is a page.
A luminous page.
Vellum. Thick. The richest ivory vellum.
A page so luscious it pulls words from out the air
like sticky flypaper hanging in a window
of a country store deep in the mountains,
holding the restless words against their struggles,
until they fly free. To tumble and summersault
through the sky, mating like birds to create
their own new messages—sent drifting down.
They twinkle and flutter around a unique person
who happens to be sitting alone when they
whirl by. They stop, and turn, and turn again
until they rest in lines on a page.
On richest vellum.

If There Is Not Love There Is Nothing

A nameless road coils inside my head
Waiting for a dream to take me
On its mystic route again,
Crooked like a snake's path across a dusty plain.

The world is yet a brighter place with snakes,
The charmed fear of coming close
To sweet temptation,
And walking in the morning
The unjudged winding ways of dreams.

A snake may slide into your pleasant garden.
A tiny moth can crash your house of cards.

So let us love each other now,
We may not meet in heaven.
Who knows the universes grace may span?
And this dear earth,
This spinning core of life,
Cannot stroll us together
Down this magic road again.

Reflections On A Seventy Year Marriage

A Novel

You in a rented tuxedo,
me on my father's arm,
he, alone, gives me to you
while my mother, dressed in lace,
sits silent in a front pew.
From the father to the husband's care;
the minister calls us man and wife,
not husband and wife.
The music, flowers, cake,
the honeymoon, oh, the honeymoon,
settling in, babies who turn to men and women
through broken bones, late night phone calls, two from police.
Society changes for women;
I choose the old title—housewife—
accepting diapers, drudge, cleaning
the same space again and again.
A hot meal when you come home.
Snickers from my modern friends.

You succeed, your fingers write your thoughts.
I read your writing, hear your fishing, hunting memories.
I learn and love you in your young days
when I didn't know you, as I love you now.

The children leave, leaving me lonely, looking
to school, decisions, a career. Time dulls our senses.

A ship and a ship
we pass and pass in our empty house.
I turn away
from you
looking for love
or a caring touch.

When eyes have turned toward other loves
and sleep is back to back for anger
then, even then, soul fingers touch.

I know you have walked through your wall of pain
to reach to me again
when, in our kitchen on a certain morning
after a certain night,
you smile across your coffee cup
and pour mine.
I sit with you. We talk
as other times. Yet not as other times
for every action has changed
the color of the air between us.
Duller or brighter.
You, wise one, choose brighter.
You make our marriage forever;
your deep love, mine deeper now.
The hurt, forgiven, forms strands of silk
acting to create another fabric
a tougher, softer weave of love.

Trips to fill your bucket, mine, ours
add happy days. Driving through beauty,

getting lost,
short comments drift through easy silence,
some thoughts shared, some not.

We leave the empty house to
live beside a loved lake.

Time carries us to age
with oatmeal breakfasts,
slower walks on softer paths.
A small stroke stiffens my left arm,
clenches my hand.
You wrap yourself around me,
bend above me,
and the struggle is easier .
I smile thinking of
how you, so sweetly awkward,
help me dress.
You still forget sometimes
to put my left arm in first.

Some good deeds bring us pleasure;
we hope to go to our heaven together
like Baucis and Philemon
but know it won't be so.
My friend, my love,
one of us will be alone
before we meet again…

Just hold my body close to yours.
to bless our memory.

On Waking From A Dream

It isn't him. It's not his eyes
nor nose, nor mouth. He isn't dressed
the way he dressed. But when I dream
of one who climbs the winding road
before me, and knows the way
to find the hidden hole that lets us in or out
of that old shell filled cave, who knows
which Indian tribe once lived here
below the mother mountains,
and where the river runs into the earth,
I know that it is him. He has returned, wanting
at least for a while, the world
we made together more than Paradise.

If Love Were Wine

I would serve you wine,
Created of grapes gathered from
Vines that grow where gods have walked,
Stirring the soil with steps of their golden feet.

I would serve you
Dressed in shimmering mist,
Holding the chalice to you
In my curved hands;
A crystal bowl so thin
It shatters after your last swallow
To send a spray high toward heaven.

A Borrowed Poem

I took the book of poems today.
I called on you and you were not at home.
You had left it on your front porch,
and rain was beating across the tall grass toward it.
Now, in my favorite chair, cuddling
a cup of hot chocolate against the drear chill,
I find a place marked as a writer marks;
a wilted plum flower.
The poem you marked says to me,
'this is why she can tell you,
although she doesn't rush it,
it is all right with her world
if she dies tomorrow.'

The Underground River

It bores its way through the earth
quiet and dark,
carrying only the load of detritus
created by its own burrowing
against the sides of its tunnel.
Untouched by the clash of swords,
guns, cannons and bombs above it,
hidden to churning crowds,
the outpouring pain
of loving and hating.

Someone was born above the river.
She lived and died above the river,
through years of unrewarded work
and unreturned nurture,
morning sun and evening darkness,
never imagining
the cool rich peace below her
flowing along
silently.

Laura, After Dying

By now, she has explained to St. Paul
Where he went wrong in denigrating women
(She will do it lovingly.)

I heard her say, once, that Jesus
Came to teach us how to live,
Not how to die.
She has thanked Him now, knowing
He came for both.

Having spoken
To a few soul companions,
She has started a conversation
With St. John of Patmos Island,
That will last for several hundred years.

I Danced

I danced that night with Apollo
While Pan played the pipes.
Sweet pipes; they curled around us,
Warm grass embraced our bare feet;
Flowers gave up their aroma,
Sent petals to flick in our hair,
Flying away as we whirled
Through the spinning blue light of fireflies,
And the waving stems of bamboo.
The pipes sang 'dance faster, dance harder'
For tomorrow stands in the shadows
Holding the scrolls of judgment,
Reading the punishment listed;
Two hundred years for the dancing,
One hundred years for each kiss.
I danced that night with Apollo.

Knowing Her

He didn't tell her
he knew her more deeply;
than a lover.
He didn't tell her
that knowing her naked words
went deeper than making love.
He didn't tell her
that when she left him
she left more of herself
on a crumpled sheet
of paper than she took with her.

Silence

If I can find a silence in my soul;
A soft retreat beyond the angry press
Of twinkling cymbals I'll remold me, whole.
I'll build a bulwark from this listlessness,
And learn again to care if one weak child
In Africa must beg for bread and die.
Again that brave, anachronistic, wild
Last fight in China's square will make me cry.
But I am filled with bright and noisy shards
Of sound and sight. They dull my empathy.
No screams but mine crush through that shroud which guards
My soul and kills the self I want to be.
I'll waste my days a doll unless I find
A silent place to clarify my mind.

Decoration Day

Let the children play
Above my body,
Let them hunt Easter eggs and throw snowballs.
And let the grown-ups
Eat pulled pork-sandwiches and potato salad
On Decoration Day, and in the fall
When they meet to clean the graveyard.
Let the grass grow above me
Tall enough to move in the wind,
And sometimes on moonlit nights
Let lovers come alone,
To walk and kiss and love
And plan their future.
Pile wildflowers on my grave
And let them stay there, fading,
Till they decay and drift into the ground
To scent my bones.

Numinous: A Word

Oxford English Reference Dictionary;
1. Indicating the presence of a divinity
2. Spiritual 3. Awe inspiring.

It is a light giving word;
A point shimmering through trees
Slanting from a light house over sail lined ships,
Glistening in a morning sunrise
Glowing under the shadows of a midnight moon;
A lamp in a curtained window
Floating angels with amber colored eyes.
A remembering word;
Soft seacoast sand against your feet,
Brown seed in an old Mason jar,
A look between strangers,
First bare feet on grass in the spring.
Apple wood in a fireplace.
The shape of a tender leaf.
A silky soft cover on a sultry night.

Blood Moon

The color of a shadow rules the sky.
Below, the psychics cry the night to come;
The end of ages
Crashing all the points of light
Into a spaceless hollow.

And ages end when...
What if God and Lucifer
Grow tired of twisting history
To endless scenes of war,
Pushing their bodiless fights onto
Bodies with different colored hands, carrying guns
And bombs and hearts to burst;
Splashing shadows of blood
Against every moon?

What if God sends a breath,
A swirl of ether through the universe,
Leading us back to love?

A Dream Of Time Removed

You find me at ocean's edge
our bare feet on cool sand.
You ask me why
I only choose the broken shells.
I say because they are like me
inside their core, the jagged scars
my fingers touch.
You hold me silently,
and lie with me for one long night.
When you go back into your mists,
when stars slip to darkness,
we leave our love shape on the sand
as bed for other lovers.

Evening At Fox Hollow Inn

Come to the fire pit made round
with fitted stones. Look to the stars
dripping light. See the constellations
move over the sky. Out on the mountain
just at the edge of our yard a coyote howls
and two more answer from the mountain top.
A deer is trapped between them. It may be just
a fawn.They sing the merciless songs of nature.
The mountain was old when it was created out of
ancient rocks and soil pressed high toward the sky.
Trees and vines hide the coyote, deer, turkey, skunk
possums, rabbits, snakes, owls, squirrels, redbirds
and the slave built stone fence that is all that
is left at the home of pioneers of unknown
names who lived in the valley below us.
The bees in their hives are sleeping.
Come closer to the fire. The wind
is cooling. Watch the faint light
tracing the mountain top.
Promising tomorrow.

The Old Book

I found it in an old book store,
The one on Ellis Street.
You know it. You walk between two buildings,
Open the door and the vintage scent of books
Splashes across your memory.
It was in one of the little back alcoves
Tucked between Greek Myths and a memoir.
The cover was puffy soft. It gave a little to my fingers,
The pages curled, with tiny splits
Here and there. Marked twenty-five cents,
It was a small volume of short stories
Published in Nineteen and Twenty Seven.
The bio in the back said the long forgotten author
Was writing a novel. I bought the book
To save it. I placed it on my shelves
Between one of Joseph Campbell's
Works on the hidden meanings of myths
And The Best American Poetry.

Driving Past An Old Graveyard in the North Georgia Mountains

There isn't time to stop and read the names,
But the shape of the stones tell me
The early gold rushers lie here
Across from the rowdy river
Summersaulting down the mountain,
Playing hopscotch over its stones,
Carrying in neutral commission
Rocks, snakes, leaves, dirt,
And the bright yellow nuggets
To their gold hungry hands.

On this same mountain the Cherokee
People, herded like animals
Started in carriages, wagons, on horses, walking,
On that long journey to the west.
Look! See them moving off,
That long line stringing out,
They aren't hungry yet. They aren't cold,
The children haven't died.
They are only confused,
Perhaps relieved to get away from the
Hot crowded stockades
Where they have been kept caged
For a whole summer.

Now starts the walking, walking all day,
Sharing, if lucky, time on a horse or wagon
Now starts the dying,
Measles, pneumonia, where are the doctors?
Hear their mourning song
From here to Oklahoma.

The persons under these grave stones
Spread over the land the Cherokees left.
They found what De Soto searched for,
Three hundred years of evolution didn't change
The pitiless clutch for gold and land.
These aren't the names of pioneers
For the land they took was planted
By the Cherokees. History makes it hard
To respect the names on these stones
As much as these Cherokee names…

Dahlonega… Chattahoochee… Etowah…Nantahala…
Ellijay…Tallulah…Chatooga…Nacoochee…Hiawassee…
…Tugaloo… Chattanooga….Coosawatie…Oothcaloga…

The Poem

It is there
saying what it says,
meaning what it means,
using words that arouse you.
Not caring if you look for meaning
that shouts to the world,
the poem speaks to you alone,
using one word of one line that draw from your
memories...good or bad,
moving you along a river path
or across faint desert footprints.
The poem grows within you
its own roots...unpruned...unwatered.
Don't think you can ever walk away
leaving it in a closed drawer
of your mind.

CPSIA information can be obtained
at www.ICGtesting.com
Printed in the USA
LVHW042101271018
595086LV00001B/2/P

9 781628 801613